# ABIEGAIL ROSE

# The Carter Effect

### How Beyoncé and Jay-Z showed me how to turn Pain and Passion to Profits.

·SINCE 1986·

**Billingslea**
**PRODUCTIONS**

First published by Billingslea Productions in 2018

First edition

ISBN: 978-1-387-92565-0

This book was professionally typeset on Reedsy.
Find out more at reedsy.com

# Contents

# PART I

# The Carter Effect Road Map

*You don't have to be the most popular, the most beautiful, the most educated, or even have the most money; your qualifications to reach your full potential is your life experiences channeling your pain into a sincere passion to succeed. My musical playlist consists of Beyoncé and Jay Z, but on one day as I listened to them share their pain, journey, and life experiences, their message shaped me and help me to channel my own pain into passion and profit. Hopefully, by sharing the advice that I have learned by listening to them, you will also discover how to!*

## One

## The Carter Effect

We can all admit that whether by sheer luck or by amazing business insight Beyoncé and Jay-Z have been capitalizing on the American public's passion for tea and turned it into a profit. If you remember back in 2014 right after what has been endearingly termed, 'Elevator-gate', whispers of Jay-Z cheating on Beyoncé with "Becky with the good hair" started.

Whether you followed the scandal across multiple news networks, The ShadeRoom, TMZ, or some form of social media you pretty much knew about it. Even if you say, well I didn't put money in their pockets, you still either heard about Elevator-Gate or Beyoncé or Jay-Z in some area of your life, no one in America is immune to their name. That in and of itself is phenomenal branding and business positioning.

Beyoncé and Jay-Z are record breaking, cash reeling phenoms. You heard about Beyoncé when she dropped Lemonade, you heard about her when she did the Super Bowl, you heard about it when Jay-Z refused to do the Super Bowl, you heard about them as a couple for On The Run Tour, you heard about Beyoncé when she broke the internet after taking a picture with their new twins, you heard about Beyoncé when she broke every record imaginable for Coachella, and you heard about Jay-Z when he dropped his album 4:44, you heard about them as a couple yet again when they announced their On The Run Tour 2, and then yet again when they dropped their joint album, Everything is Love, while on said tour.

Even if you haven't supported them in any of these endeavors you have heard about them performing these fetes and that means their brand and their business is strong. So strong that it by passes racial, sexual, and financial barriers. Put on Single Ladies in the club and you'll see a mish mash of people dancing to it, hitting every step on beat, owning every lyric as if they wrote it themselves.

If you think I'm wrong. Picture your favorite actor. I'm a bonafide awkward black girl and mine's is Julia Roberts, Ms. Pretty Woman herself. Truth be told even though she is an amazing actress, I know nothing about her or even that she had two movies drop over the last couple of years. With the Carter's however, it's a different story, whether you are a fan, stan, or hater – you are AWARE, which gives them the potential to profit off of you!

It's 'Business and Branding by Design', The Carter's own The Blueprint to it and have it made it into something that very few people can imitate. There are not too many other who have stumbled across this treasure map of turning pain into purpose, turning pain in promise, or turning pain into profit.

But you can see examples in others like Adele and Mary J Blige, who sing from their souls about hurts that's makes us cry with them even when things in our own relationships are going well. Tyler Perry and Tiffany Haddish who both went through a tragic bout of homelessness from which they turned the pain of that situation into laughter, laughter that they have in turn gifted us with.

So, what exactly has Beyoncé and Jay-Z accomplished and what made my third eye pop open in realization of the potential for a better me?

Well as I worked out, which I rarely do, I had on Lemonade, followed by 4:44, and capped it their newly released joint album, Everything is Love. As I listened to these complete albums in succession it hit me. Beyoncé and Jay-Z have monetized relationship problems, their pain, to the tune of hundreds of millions of dollars.

I'm going to lay it down for you with the thousand-foot view and then show you how you can use the same blueprint The Carter's have, to turn your own pain into profits.

So, what started off this unfortunate chain of painful events, which turn into something so magnificent that it spawned 3 albums, 2 world tours, and 1 set of twins? 'Elevator-Gate'.

In 2014 while leaving a Met Gala afterparty, Beyoncé, Jay-Z, and Solange were caught on elevator surveillance. The footage showed Solange and Jay-Z getting into an argument and then Solange getting her Houston, TX on and throwing them bows as she wildly hit and kicked him, before being separated by what appeared to be security and Beyoncé. Of course, in this modern age there are no secrets, so once TMZ got their hands on the footage, that was all she wrote. This kicked the rumor mill into high gear. Everybody and they mama wants to know: who is this woman that has Solange beating Jay-Z up over? Who is Becky?

After that Beyoncé kept us all talking when she debuted a remix of her song "Flawless" that seemed to reference the famous elevator brawl.

*"Of course, sometimes shit goes down when there's a billion dollars on an elevator..."*

This really sent the Rumor Mill into overdrive and then she drops her album Lemonade, and the floodgates opened.

Not only did Mrs. Carter release her album Lemonade, but she released it with a full Visual Album, then a new HBO special, and a Super Bowl performance. She broke records what the album, makes money off that, and then goes on Formation World Tour. Most of which is music relating to their relationship problems. They have essentially made the pain of their relationship into a business which is producing mega profits.

After I realized how the Carter's had accomplished this and implemented it into my own life, I wanted to share this with you to allow you channel your own pain or set backs into profit or passion. To make it easy, I have broken it down for you into easy five steps.

1. Make 'Lemonade' and decide to no longer be a victim.
2. It's '4:44' get clear on what you want and what you'll sacrifice to get it.
3. Go 'On The Run' and take progressive action.
4. Silence your giants and tell them 'Everything Is Love'.
5. Don't stop! Go 'On The Run 2' find smart ways to be profitable!

Anyone that is interested in finding true success throughout their lives can do so, with the right tools, the right amount of ambition and the knowledge to make it all happen. **Yet, the entrepreneur or originator (write, singer, musician, teacher, engineer, etc.), no matter what field they are in must plan and find success through much more than just these things.**

# Two

# My Advice To You

To be successful, you are not just looking for benefits right now. While you are sure to want what you are passionate about to truly take off and do well in its first year, its infancy, it is just as important, if not more so, that the long-term goals you have match the need that you have as well.

In the long term, a successful person's world is much different and much more unique. To find true success, you need to think of today as well as tomorrow, two-fold.

How and what will you do to ensure that your BUSINESS or TALENT, the one that you have worked so hard to make happen in the first place, is going to make it in the long term? Although this is not something easy to do, you can do it with proper planning and preparation.

In this book, I will share what I have learned from watching and listening to Beyoncé and Jay-Z. Which are some of the most essential principles for protecting your BUSINESS or TALENT not only for today, but the long term.

As a new or aspiring businessperson, you don't not think about what the future will hold because only today matters. Yet, now is the perfect time to step back and to find out, what is the best way to manage your business for the long term.

If you wish to have a business or passion that allows for success and long-term profits, then it is essential that you spend some time now planning for it to happen.

**The good news is that you do not have to go to school or be a rocket scientist to figure this out. In fact, just read this book as you listen to Lemonade, 4:44, and Everything Is Love on repeat.**

Of course, I also hope you are inspired to take the next step, break whatever barrier is keeping you from reaching your full potential, deal with your pain, and to find the true benefit of your business, art-form, passion, etc. by putting these things steps into action first and foremost. When you do these things, you will truly be able to turn your pain into profits.

I may not like all the music that Beyoncé and Jay-Z have dropped, but even someone who refuses to recognize the brand they've established for themselves must acknowledge they've been feeding us lyrical business gems for a while. Take for instance Jay's verse on the Remix to Kanye West's song Diamonds from Sierra Leone.

*"The pressure's on, but guess who ain't gon' crack? ... Difficult takes a day, impossible takes a week... I'm not a businessman, I'm a business, man. Let me handle my business, damn!"*

# PART II

# Make 'Lemonade' and Decide to No Longer Be a Victim

*Lemonade was Beyoncé's yell that she would no longer be a victim and accept infidelity so Jay-Z needed to get it together or hit the door.*

*Do like Bey and Decide to No Longer to be a Victim to whatever has caused you pain, but instead own it!*

*Now, it is not my intention to belittle or minimize any kind of pain you may have been experienced. Whether business or personal pain, there will come a day that you will have to face it, get closure and decide to move forward. Deciding to not be a victim doesn't mean your pain isn't real, it simply means that you refuse to allow the experience or pain to hold you captive.*

## Three

# The Pain of Today Isn't Everything, Really!

*Lesson from Beyoncé*

What I like about Beyoncé is that when Elevator-Gate happened, instead of doing like most women do and burying their head in the sand or harming herself she faced it head on and make a whole entire album about it. Every lyric on every track, from "Pray You Catch Me" to "Hold Up" to "Sand Castles," was analyzed for clues, and the consensus was that Beyonce had caught Jay-Z in a betrayal, almost left him, but ultimately chose to stay after a hell of a reckoning. And obviously there would be no follow-up interviews to clarify or further confirm whatever information was gleaned from that album. Essentially marketing her pain. She said, whelp it happened, everybody knows, might as well tell my side of the story, somebody can relate to it, and get paid in the process. Honey it worked.

I'm a writer and I've been through so much in life from being kidnapped and raped by an ex-boyfriend, being a single mother, flunking out college due to depression, going bankrupt, and getting a divorce. I thought that all that pain defined me, sullied me, stagnated me, limited me. But when I saw this woman; who essentially to me, already had everything and was still experiencing some of the same problems that I had, I was in awe! Because not only did she rise above it, but she owned, strengthened her brand off it, and profited from it, I was in awe!

Listening to her album and watching her perform helped me to burst out of the shadows of my own past. I started to notice a change in me, I didn't shrink away when someone asked me about my past, I pushed my shoulders back and told them the truth and then turned the conversation into a selling point of my good qualities and accomplishments. I started doing that with everything. I started using that pain I had inside to create new characters, new lyrics, and pushed away my reluctance to share them, but instead started daring myself to aim higher.

Daring myself to aim higher, is how I landed a nine book publishing contract. I dared myself to stop being scared, own my writing, and submit my work to publishers. I also started stop treating my talent as a HOBBY but as a BUSINESS.

*How You Can Do This*

**Realize that the Pain you feel Today Isn't Everything, Really!**

As an entrepreneur or originator, your job is very detailed. You need to be the creative one. You need to be the boss. You need to hold the vision of your business at the head of each and everything that you do for that business. But, today isn't everything.

As a business owner (you are a business owner - your talent and your craft is your business), you must remember the fact that the long-term goals and process of your business can only happen if you plan for it now, not in the day.

You have probably heard people tell you that you need to; "Live in the day!" As an entrepreneur or originator, this is not possible and should not be the way that you hold your business agenda.

*But, why not?*

Most of the time, we would like to think that all we really need to do is to put together a plan and hold onto it. Somehow, things will fall into place. It must. That's all it can do.

Yet, from a business standpoint, there is much more to think

15

about.

For example, you may have employees that need the funds that come from your business for their day to day expenses.

You may need to take into consideration the overall benefits that you have in keeping your business going. What about your assets? Will they make it through the process? How about your cash flow? What will happen if something does go wrong?

All these things are only the tip of the iceberg when it comes to ruining a business in the long term. The bottom line is that you need to consider what your business will be like today as well as ten, twenty and more years down the road.

## Think About This

Before we get started, it is essential that you understand two concepts of your business dealings. When you make a decision in your business, ask yourself these questions first and foremost.
- When I make this decision, what is the short term and immediate effects of doing so? How does this affect my business today?
- When I make this decision, what is the long-term effect of making this choice? How will this decision affect my business months and years from now?

When you take the time to carefully consider decisions that happen in front of you, you put yourself in charge of your destiny.

If you allow the cards to fall where they may, you may not be in business six months from now. Therefore, as you work through this book, ask yourself what steps you can take right now that will better your overall business in the short and the long term.

Of course, we should mention that there is never a for sure way to know what the future holds. There is no way to know if you are really making the right decision or not. But, what you must do here is to ensure that you give tomorrow the best possible chance that you can.

Don't let it just happen, make today count for tomorrow and tomorrow's tomorrow too.

**Four**

# Know Your Past, So You Won't Repeat It!

O ne thing that many business owners do not take into account enough is their history and learning from it. When you consider how your history affects your future potential, you can better see why it is essential for this to be something you pay a good amount of attention to.

Do you learn from history?

Many of us will recall the times when our parent's scolded us. "Don't do that again!" "Learn from your mistakes." All of these things are very important in the business world as well.

In this principal that is crucial to your business's success, you do need to take into consideration your past and where it has been to help you to figure out where you and your business are going.

Questions To Consider

Now, to get started with this principal, take into consideration these questions.

1. Where have you been and what have you learned? When you think about the past, determine just what it means to find success in this way. What background do you have that has taught you something that could play a role in your life and well being today?

2. What have you learned from mistakes? Every entrepreneur makes mistakes as they are working through their business. No matter if you are brand new or a seasoned pro, mistakes can happen one time for many reasons. But, the difference is if you allow it to happen again. If not, then you can find success much easier and faster than if you repeat the same mistake time and time again.

3. What do you wish you would have done differently? Regrets do not have to be wasted this time. As an entrepreneur, you may have several regrets in mind. Perhaps you feel as if you have lost a great deal of time getting your business up and running. Now, take this regret and determine what you would do today. Would you start your business sooner? Put more into it sooner?

Understanding these aspects of your past can help you in the long term. Of course, we do not want to keep making the same mistakes, but there are not many business owners that do this.

Instead, most of us will learn from our mistakes but only if we take the time to look at them and see what they were and how they could be avoided.

Your history is solely yours. Whether you look at a personal life history and your business or just the business alone, it is essential to stop and look and learn.

Making mistakes today is not easy to do. No one wants to do it, but if it does happen to you, do the following.

1. Recognize that something did not go right. Do not get angry about it (if possible!) and realize that something went wrong.

2. Determine what it was and determine how it happened. Getting the full story, learning the whole puzzle will allow for better understanding. Learning how it happened allows you to see in full detail what the mistake was.

3. Decide to improve your chances of not letting that mistake happen again. To do this, insure that you spend the necessary time making decisions to avoid this problem.

All Histories Are Not Bad

It is important to note that history does not always have to tell you the bad side of things. You can and you should see the good things that have happened in your history as well. What was it that got you to this success level that you are at today? What was it that makes that first sale happen and happen so well?

Taking a look at the good things that have happened in the past is part of the principal of looking to the past for answers of your future. They allow you to see a true benefit to the good that has happened in your business. You may even be able to take note of the way that the good has happened to make it happen again and again into your business's future as well.

When you take the time to analyze all of the good and the bad that has happened in your past, you can make sure that the benefits come through in the future while the mistakes do not.

As part of your future success, you must understand your history and how to secure the future through this huge amount of knowledge that you have. Believe it or not, this is a personal touch and experience no one else can have.

# PART III

# It's '4:44', so Get Clear on What You Want and What You'll Do To Get It!

*Jay-Z knew that he was in danger of losing his family after cheating and his album 4:44 is a confessional and clear request for a new martial chapter.*

*Now that you are beginning a new chapter, it's critically important that you are precise and intentional on WHY you want to use "pain" to bring some greater benefit. For ex: If you were in a bad relationship, perhaps you want to help other avoid the same pitfalls you fell into. Or if you were a dropout, but you still found success in business and what t help those who feels their lack of education makes them unqualified to be an entrepreneur.*

Five

# Grow & Stay Relevant!

When you are green, you are growing. Once you start to turn red, you are expiring. Don't you want to always stay green then?

As an entrepreneur, one thing that you should realize is that the world never stays the same. You are, for the most part, always going to find some changes happening. As a business owner, if you can not adjust your business to those changes, you may find yourself facing more problems then benefits.

Many companies have had to go out of business simply because their product no longer works with what the consumer needs. It does not matter what type of business you have either. The bottom line is that if you are not green and growing, you are not going to make it in business for long.

Is your business green and growing?

The Long Term Goal

The long term goal of any business situation is to insure that they are able to meet the needs of the client or consumer. If they can not do this, they can not have consumers and will eventually fall out of the scope. If they do happen to do this, they will find rewards continuously with increased profit and new customers to fill their pockets.

In this case, the long term goal that you need to make is to maintain green. You need to maintain some aspect that will continuously help you to move forward with what is happening within your business.

If you are not sure why this is important, take for instance, the current situation.

Enter The Car Manufacturing Business

Today, we hear quite a bit of talk about energy cost, the cost of gas and all that goes with it. In fact, today, more people know what the cost of a barrel of crude oil is than they ever have. Why is this; and what does this do for the industry?

If you haven't spent any time shopping or a car, you may not realize that many manufacturers are struggling to stay in business. Their problem is that their cars, trucks or anything in between are not able to meet the demands of the consumer.

Why not? They may not be able to offer low enough mileage.

With each passing year, more and more consumers are looking for a better way to fuel their energy needs. That comes in the way of cars that are hybrids and those that do not run on gas at all.

In these cases, if the business can not meet the needs of the consumer, how can they run effective businesses?

They can't and that is the same thing that can happen to virtually any business out there. Unless your business can be green, growing and exploring new routes to take, it can not meet the needs of the consumer who is, of course, the lifeblood of the business.

How To Do It

The question that you need to ask yourself, then, is what do you need to do to make this happen in your business?

Let's say that you have an internet business. Perhaps one of the important things that you must do is keep up with search engine optimization.

If you do not follow and keep in contact with the new rules and the changing scheme of matters, your website won't rank well and will fall out of the scope of being worthwhile.

In this case, it is essential that you maintain the ability to keep your knowledge and your skill at the highest quality. The same goes for various other businesses including those such as insurance agency and real estate agency. Unless you keep your knowledge at the top, you can not make sure you are doing what is right.

There are other ways that you need to think about this as well. For example, what about marketing? If your marketing is not trendy enough (or happens to be too trendy for the wrong market) you may find yourself in trouble.

In this case, it is essential for you to find a way to target the right audience with the right medium and to keep it up. You already know how to market your business; just make sure that you stay up to date on how to do this as the market changes.

What other aspects of your business can you think of that have the same potential for your attention?

Finding the various ways that you need to stay fresh may include keeping your business product fresh, with the latest technology and aspects to fit the consumer's need and even reinventing yourself to insure that the company always stays at the top.

When you invest time and money into keeping yourself green, the business always has the potential for success.

Understanding The Ever Changing Consumer

One of the most difficult things that you will need to do as an entrepreneur is to insure that you meet your consumers needs. What is difficult about this is not the fact that you need to do it, but rather how you go about understanding your consumer.

Some companies spend millions of dollars on research each year to insure that their product or that their sales pitch will be well received by the economy. The scary factors is that even with all of that, they are still risking a lot and often they do fail at what they are doing.

This can leave the small entrepreneur left to wonder how in the world they can afford to make this happen.

Understanding the consumer is not an easy task. It is essential that someone work hard to finding this information though.

If you are interested, you can do this through hiring a company to do your marketing research. This can be a solid decision that is provided at a decent cost to you. Depending on your specific business and your product, as well as your marketing budget, this may be a good option for you.

On the other hand, it may not be something that you wish to pursue. In that case, it is essential that you invest some time in finding the right solution through other means. No matter what you do from talking with your customers individually to watching market trends in what your competition does, the goal is to insure that you keep offering the best product possible.

To make sure that you are green, compare what you have to offer to the consumer's other choices. What do they have that makes them a better choice over you?

When you can answer that and then tackle that, you will be green and growing, growing towards profits of course.

## Six

# Manage Your Growth and Your Dollars!

W hat makes you profitable as a business owner? In the next chapter, we will look at the ways in which you must manage your cash flow and assets if you plan to have money in your pocket in the long term.

Do you have the ability to think about, analyze and then finally decide on business related decisions?

As we have discussed, your ability to do these things is what will hold you back or launch you forward today as well as well into the future. Now, take those ideas and determine just how well they fit into your ability to make decisions about your business success where it counts: the profit margin.

Throughout this chapter will we will talk about several aspects in detail, allowing you to fully understand what you need to do to be successful in regards to your business's profitability.

## Controlling Your Money, Correctly

Do you have what it takes to manage your money? If not, it is time to find someone that can and will do it for you. Without tight control over the finances in your business, there is no telling what the future may or may not hold. That does not mean that you can not spend money. This is a huge mistake that people make.

Instead, as the entrepreneur and business owner, you need to learn to spend money the right way instead.

The first thing for you to do is to determine a budget for your business success. This should be an overall budget at first. Things to consider include:

· Managing expenses that will continue to keep the business up and running well.

· Managing your business's debt due to growth or to start up costs (to pay them down successfully.)

· Managing profit to if available must be done with an idea of how much will be spent on investing back into the business and what will go towards other beneficial needs the business has.

The budget should be done carefully, with a good deal of thought placed on each of these areas. Instead of a dollar mount, the budget of the business should be done by percentages.

Perhaps 20 percent of the profit will go towards investment back into the business whereas the rest of the profit will go to paying down debt. Whatever percentages you are comfortable with should be taken into consideration here.

Beyond the budget aspect of managing funds is the strictly organization aspects that need to be taken care of. Good quality, detailed accounting and bookkeeping needs to be done to manage the business's overall success and funds to a T.

In addition, there needs to measures put in place to manage unexpected expenses and even just making sure that everything is accounted for.

Although this seems obvious to note, plenty of businesses fail because of poor money management in the beginning stages. Do not get caught in the "I don't have time now, I will do it later" scam. Without doing this from the beginning, it will not happen throughout your business.

Don't Think You Need To?

If you do not think that you need to do this type of detailed accounting of your business, you are setting yourself up for a big failure. Now, that is not to say that you can not make a profit by being sloppy, but remember, we are talking about the long term here.

Even very large, international companies are very careful about where every penny that they spend goes. After all, this is money that could be doing something for the business, right? It does not matter if you have hundreds of dollars to budget or billions, tight money management is the key to successfully funding any business through good and bad times.

In addition, make sure you are monitoring these numbers as well. It does not do you any good to put in place a system and to use it but not to utilize it to the fullest extent. The fact is that you should be doing these things:

· Determine where money is going and if it is being done accurately.

· Determine where you can cut back in costs and expenses.

· Determine what you can do differently for less funds so without jeopardizing the actual quality of your business.

Being a bit tight wadded with your business is not a bad thing, assuming that you take care of all aspects of the business's need including reinvesting and growth potential as well.

Your Cash Flow

The next money management principal that you need to take into consideration is that of your cash flow. Without having a good amount of cash flow in your business, it will sink.

If you are a small business owner, it is even more important to do this simply because there is nothing and no one behind you to support that bad year or that big accident that has happened. Loans are only so good and they are not any good if you can not get them.

The ability to maintain your cash flow is the key to having a successfully and long term business. Without your careful management of cash flow, your business will not make it through leaner times or even the better times for that matter.

How do you do this? There are several things that you need to take into consideration here.

First off, you should make sure that as the entrepreneur you have a good strong hand in the cash flow of your business. You should be able to personally monitor it each and every day.

Does this sound like too much? If you do not do this, you can not possibly know where your business stands on any given day. That can lead to potential long term problems with your success.

Carefully consider each and every expenditure that you make. As an entrepreneur, you need to make these decisions wisely. Just as growing too fast can hurt you, so can not having the cash flow to support your business in the short or long term can.

In addition, you should personally monitor your budget, your expenses, your profit and your ability to use every dollar that you have wisely. That is what you have those budgets in place for, after all. Use them, keep at them and work each dollar to get the most out of it.

## Two Principles To Remember

When it comes to business success, you will need to consider these two principles as far as how money management goes.

First, consider this: You should only be spending money when there is a potential to earn money from that expense.

It is self explanatory, isn't it? You should not be making an investment in your business, especially a small business owner, unless it will allow you to make more money as the end and direct result.

Secondly, consider this: "If it is not revenue, it is an expense."

How does that play into the business that you are currently running? Does it offer you the ability to make ends meet successfully? Do you make purchases without careful thought about those dollars? If it is not revenue to you, it is an expense.

Managing your cash flow successfully will allow your business to bank funds instead of to loose funds. When you do this successfully, your business has the potential to be a long term success. If you want to be there in the future, manage your cash successfully, with an eye on just about every dollar you have.

Its Not Being Cheap, Its Being Smart

Although it may sound like we are telling you to be frugal or cheap with your business, you need to insure that the funds that you are spending will be funds that are spent wisely, without waste.

How should you be frugal (that's a better name for it!) so much so that you will be able to find true success from doing so?

· Determine how you spend every dollar of your business's budget.

· Is that dollar being spent the best way that it can be? Does whatever it is being spent on benefit your bottom line?

· IS there a better way to spend that dollar? Can you get more for it with another company or service or another opportunity?

· Is there a way to save your money better, with a better return on it?

These are questions that any business owner should be considering each and every day that he owns his business. What can he do better to save more in his business for his business?

Why do this?

How many millionaires or even billionaires have you heard of that still drive their old, beat up cars? Why do they do that when they can afford to have much more beautiful and expensive cars?

It is not because they do not want to spend money or that they like being cheep. The benefit here actually comes from the fact that they like to save. Saving cash for your business is a great way to find true success because you will have those funds to use time and time again when you do need them.

The founder of Wal-Mart, Sam Walton, was worth $25 billion dollars at one point in his career. Would you believe that even with that type of worth he still drove his old, pick up truck into the job each day? Being frugal has its rewards as this is obviously what led him to having a net worth of $25 billion dollars.

When you are frugal, your business will prosper, year after year. If you are a spender, you won't have the funds to allow that to happen year after year, will you?

All of these money savings and cash handling tips may not seem like that big of a deal to you. If that is the case, you are already doing them and finding success with it, or you are actually wasting money and not achieving the success that you already want.

Yet, managing your funds wisely is one of the key components to your success in a small business. Every entrepreneur must take the time to do this or they will find themselves without the benefits that they need so badly.

In the end, is it worth being a bit frugal to reach that huge, multi billion dollar net worth? There is no car in this world that can make that type of promise to you, can it?

Make sure you install these money managing benefits and principals into your daily routine and long term goals within your business.

# PART IV

# Go 'On The Run' and Take Progressive Action!

*Do like the Carter's. After it was all said and done - they decided staying together was their vision and profit center so they implemented the On The Run tour.*

*Now that you have your vision in place, ask yourself what the next steps are to make it happen. The powerful thing about action is that it continues the healing process in you because it gives you the courage to confront and face what was once fearful and intimidating. Action is powerful and absolutely liberating.*

# Seven

# Know Who You Get Your Profits From!

One thing that we do need to mention is hat the market that you face is likely to be much different than the market that someone else faces. The goals that you have in comparison to the goals of someone else are much different. In fact, you are sure to see yourself striving for benefits that are not on target for your business.

First off, take a step back, out of the picture and look at your market.

If you are selling on the internet, look at the other sellers.

If you are a small local business owner, step back and look at your local market.

Whatever you are doing, step back.

To Consider Now

The market that you work in is very dependant on who your customers are. If you are looking for immediate success, just opening your doors can help you to get started. But, in looking at your market, you can better see several things.

Ask yourself and answer these questions before moving forward.

· Who is my customer? The seniors or the children, the business women or the business owner…determine who your customer is.

· How do they find you? Do they find you online, through a simple web search? Do they need to find you through an affiliate link? Do they find you in their local area, in one of the most popular areas in the city?

· Who else is out there? Who is your competition? Where are they located? What do they offer that allows you to better them? How do they better you in your marketplace? Why are they open, pulling business away from you?

· What do you offer that is better, in some way, then the other guy? What do they offer that is better in some way than you?

· Where is your market going? Is the economy growing, stalling out, or is it holding steady? What amount of money do your customers have to spend on your product?

You can go on and on with things that you should be considering about your own specific business. Understanding your market is crucial to understanding what your future is.

If you do not know who your consumer is, then how do you know how they are changing?

In addition, you need to know what to expect to get from the market around you. If you find that the economy is slipping, it may be quite necessary to pull back and to instead look to the future in a different way.

If you look at your market and see that your competition has taken your product in a different way and is having success with that, you need to make a move. How do you compete? What will you offer that is better? In addition, how will you take the next step into success? How will you better them?

Paying Attention Counts

By paying attention to your market, you will make better decisions. When you look towards the long term goals that you have in place to keep your business up and running, you need to make sure that your market is one of the top priorities that you have.

If you do not invest time in keeping yourself in that market-place, or even expanding out of it, you can not and will not make things work. The business can not grow or stay green without a constant watchful eye on the market around you.

In later chapters we will talk more about growth and how to envision your future in this regard. Yet, it is important to note that you need to watch your market for the signs that it needs more of your product or that it is not picking up on it.

There is no doubt that some of these things are essential to do but some may be hard to do as well. Yet, if you do not invest the time that it takes to analyze and understand the customer that you have, how in the world will you make it work?

Again, you have the ability to hire someone to do this work for you. But, you can and you should consider not only doing this but also helping yourself with your own research and know how.

Being a physical presence in your marketplace (even on the web) helps you to make sure that people can come to you. It allows you to see your market first hand and therefore make good decisions.

# Eight

# Be a Trend Setter, Not a Trend Seeker!

⚜

*I*s your business a trend setter? Or, do you follow the trend?

If you are not sure, consider how this plays a role in your future.

As a trend setter, you are always one step ahead of the game. What you do, others look up to, but not just this one time. If you can manage to do this often, setting the trend that is, you can even create the fact that you will have others looking to you to set the next trend.

On the other hand, if you are following the trend, things are not so great. You will have to make up time for the other product or business that is doing well. You have lost precious sales time in the process. In addition, you will always need to watch the other guy for what is going to happen next, instead of being in charge of what that is. This can be a challenging place to be, actually.

Take a minute now to think about where you are in this equation.

Do you tend to follow the lead of someone else, hoping that there will be enough in the pot for you too? Or, do you seek out something new and exciting and try to incorporate that into your business?

Depending on where you stand currently should help you to see just how this affects your long term goals and ability to reach the success that you want.

Long Term Trend?

We all know that trends come and go. You should also realize that not every one of them is the right way to go for each business. Yet, the trend is something to pay attention to when looking at your long term success.

As we mentioned, the benefits of setting the trend in your market place are not just based on the basics of the sale. Sure, if you can get a monopoly on a product for a few days, weeks or longer, you are going to have some awesome sales to take advantage of.

Yet, those sales are soon gone. In the short term, that is all that matters. But, in this case, we are talking about the long term goals here.

If you are the trend setter, then, your long term benefits of being in this business is that you have more ability and movement to set the next trend too.

Some companies in the market place do not have the ability to fill their customer's needs perfectly. Some will only find success once in a while when it comes to trends. Yet, the company that is able to set a few trends can secure more ability in the future to do the same.

When a company has other companies looking to them for the next trend, guess who is going to make long term success?

Consider Your Reputation

This is the one factor that plays a role in developing your reputation as a company as well. Not all companies are able to say that they have a good reputation with their consumers on a long term basis. Yet, those that do can almost count on a monopoly in their market.

Take for example the mom and pop shops that are so frequently around well past their prime. Why are these such great places to go? It's because they have a solid reputation for providing success and for doing well with their product. Even if their product is outdated, it is still something that is wanted and needed for its quality. That helps to fund true success with the market.

Of course, your reputation comes into play for more reasons

or ways than just this. The fact is that it also happens when you are considering customer service, pricing, good community connections and so on. These things all play a role in what your reputation is, just to name a few of them!

When you are considering your long term goal of success and having good money in your pocket, how does your reputation play a role?

We talked about how this happens with trend setting, but it can go further than that. In today's offline world, it is hard to get a good cup of coffee without begging. No matter if you are online or offline with your product, though, you can gain many rewards and benefits by just providing good service.

Building a reputation is essential to continued growth. Yet, remember that a reputation can go both ways (good and bad!) Therefore, make sure that you have a solid backing of pleased customers in your marketplace. It will pay off for you today as well as long into the future.

## PART V

# Silence Your Internal Haters and Tell Them Everything is Love

*Beyonce and Jay-Z let us into their personal lives with Lemonade, 4:44, and the On The Run tour. But as soon as started to get comfortable think we knew the whole story they hit us with another album this time together as The Carters called Everything is Love. Essentially putting haters in their places and letting us know they are a single unit.*

*As soon as you gain resolve and make up your mind that you are going to do something and start moving toward it, there may be challenges that come up, that's Life! No worries. Usually these internal haters(fear, procrastination, self-doubt, pity, reliving of past pain, etc.) are just roadblocks to see how badly do YOU want your dream. Gear up to face your giants head on as they come. Serve notice that they must vacate immediately, because you and your dreams are here to stay!*

# Nine

# *Invest in Your Craft*

❦

I f you are like many entrepreneurs, then you know that it is essential to have a good deal of knowledge when it comes to running your business.

As we have talked about, it is important to make sure that those that are providing you with the necessary information are doing so without taking all of your money just so that you can spend more.

For example, some of the most common mistakes the entrepreneurs that are just starting out make is that they just keep purchasing information. This is especially true of those that are starting a business online.

There is no doubt that you do need to have a good amount of knowledge to make something happen. You need to know how to get started, you need to know what steps to take and you need to know just where to do all of this. But, there is a limit.

One thing that you should take into consideration is your ability to make decisions. Once you have purchased the latest tell all kit, realize that you are ready to make some decisions.

If you purchase one kit or program and see another that seems to offer some additional benefits, you may be tempted purchase that one too. After all, it can not hurt to have some more information, can it?

It doesn't hurt to have a good amount of information, except for the pocketbook, of course. Yet, that is not the problem. What the problem is what you do with it.

A Principle

There are a number of things that you can do to make this happen to you. Remember this principle.

If you find yourself purchasing one product after another product, you are not thinking about your next productive move, but rather holding yourself up.

If you purchase a product to benefit your business, it is essential for you to use it and get the most out of it prior to moving on to the next purchase.

Making It Count

In later chapters we will talk about the fact that you need to manage your money closely, but for now, realize that the investment in any asset or tool to benefit your business needs to be used fully for it to be a wise investment.

No matter what business you are in, if you do not take the time to invest in a business product wisely, you are literally throwing your profit out.

If you fall victim to all of those ploys to purchase this greta kit or that sure fire method of making a million dollars, you sure are helping someone else to make that million dollars.

Now, that is not to say that you shouldn't purchase any of them. Instead, select the one that provides the best resources for you, invest in it wisely and then use it completely, incorporating all that needs to be incorporated into the plan.

When you do this, your investment is beneficial to your business. If you just move on to the next thing, you find yourself facing not benefits but pitfalls and an empty wallet to go with it.

Making Wise Choices

In our next chapters, we will touch on some very important assets including your cash flow. But, before we do that, we need to touch on the principal of making the right decisions regarding your business.

How do you make decisions? Do you make spur of the moment choices because that is the way that you feel that day?

Do you work hard at finding the right solution, so much so that by the time you make the decision it is too late?

If you do these things, you are not benefiting your business, but rather letting the cards fall where they will. This is a huge problem for the overwhelming majority of those entrepreneurs out there that are just starting out. Making wise decisions is not easy, but it must be done, nevertheless.

Once you realize the way that you are currently making a decision, you can begin to correct it. To help you to make the right choices, follow these steps and tips to securing the right decisions without letting them get past you.

Decision Making Tips

Making a decision is hard work. Here are some tips to help you.

1. Invest time in learning about the possible product or problem that you are facing. If you are trying to decide on whether or not to purchase a product, consider what it will do to enhance your business's performance. What can it do for you?

2. Spend some time researching possible solutions, both what you have found and what you have not. What can it do for your problem? What is the lowest cost you can find? What are the potential pitfalls of this item?

3. After this is done, determine if the investment is worth it to your own well being or to your business's. Waiting until after you learn more about the product will allow a decision to form as a conclusion to the research you have done.

4. If you can not decide within a few days, then perhaps you are too leery of this item or choice to determine it is right for your business. Let it go and forget it. Or, find another option. Do not dwell on it.

Making the right decisions also means that you need to realize your current state of affairs.

If your business is not pulling in profits because it does not have the necessary tools, it is time to invest in some new tools otherwise your business will not be there long enough for you to worry about it.

If your business is doing okay and there is no hang up, then do not invest in something that does not have a direct return on your profit margin.

Most entrepreneurs have tons of people coming to them offering them a wide range of different benefits, products, and services because, like you, they are looking to make their business work. Don't fall for these lures and savvy businessmen that think they can solve your problems.

Although it may seem difficult to make good decisions in relation to the business that you have, it is imperative that you learn to trust yourself. If you do not trust your decisions, you can not run a business.

This too is a principal that you need to realize: If you do not trust yourself, you can not ruin a successful business.

**Ten**

# Prune! So You Don't Stop Growing!

O ne of the long term things that every business owner must think about is growth.

Growth is the expansion of your business to the next level. This could mean expanding your business to include more products, to do more things, or to grow physically by adding more locations.

Growth is what holds the potential for the most success in the long term. An entrepreneur can find many benefits for themselves if they can manage to grow carefully, without going too far or stretching too thin too fast.

If that sounds difficult to do, it can be. Many businesses have failed by expanding too quickly and not having enough of the market share to hold them together. On the other hand, there are plenty of businesses out there that have not grown as much as they could and now are missing out on the potential larger profit margin.

### It's Personal Too

Of course, the growth of your business is a personal choice. Not everyone can determine where they lie here at the beginning of their business as well. Yet, one thing is sure.

Your growth potential has a lot to do with your security in your business. If you have trust and assurance that your business is a business worth existing, then by all means you can grow. If you are not sure and can not make decisions regarding the growth of your business, it can not possibly grow.

Although most people are ready and willing to take full advantage of an opportunity to build on what they have created, others are quite willing to let the pieces fall as they may.

One principle that you need to remember, then, is that to become successful in your business, you need to determine your level of security in risk. What are you comfortable with and how can you insure that what you are doing is what will pay off in the long term?

These are hard questions to answer but they must be done.

### Growing Too Fast

One of the worst things that you can do for your business is to grow too fast. If you do not have the assets and the cash flow to back up this type of major expansion, you may find yourself facing a number of problems just maintaining your business rather than worrying about expanding it.

The risk of failure due to over expanding too quickly is that you just may not be able to handle the obligations of several locations or such a large corporation. Many of the larger corporations that have faced this have fallen through because of the enormous expense of taking on another building, another payroll, another unit.

Yet, the smaller business owner does not face this huge number of risks as the larger corporation. But!

It is important to make sure that you invest wisely in growth and not without investing time first. Determining where your potential benefits are is the first key to success. In addition, a good look at what the possibilities are is in order.

Are You Ready To Grow?

Those that are interested in finding the right solution in the terms of growth are doing the right thing. Remember though that it is important to make a decision in the right frame of mind and with the right amount of research done first.

In terms of growing, what the right choice is happens to be up to you individually. Ask these questions of your success:

1. Does your business have the cash flow to support not only this functioning location (or your current business) as well as another?

2. If you are expanding, what makes you believe that this expansion will serve your business well?

3. What is the likely expense of growing and does the business have the necessary means to protecting and covering that cost?

All of these things are crucial to your business's success in the growth factor. But, you also need to insure that you do not limit your growth with not enough opportunity either.

Don't Limit It

The mistake of many business owners is that they do not put their foot out there and expand fast enough or at all. While it is essential not to move too fast, it is just as important to consider if you are moving just too slow for benefit either.

To understand this factor, you again need to turn to your business. Are you getting all that you can from it? Can you do more or get a better bottom line if you do grow in some shape?

To learn the right amount of growth for your business, you can do test market studies, invest in surveys, or just start slowly and work up to it. The amount that you put into your business is really up to you and to how well the business has been doing to this point.

A bad business that is not doing well in one location may not be able to do well elsewhere either.

A good business that is thriving may be hindered by not moving it.

Of course, the opposite is true too. Research is the best way to determine where growth stands in your business.

# PART VI

# Go Back 'On The Run 2' Find Smart Ways To Be Profitable

*We're all in business to be make money, period. The purpose often comes from our pain, in most cases lead us to our passion. And it's our passion, when we use it to solve a problem through excellent service, guarantees reward and profit in the marketplace. Let your past pain work for you. Leverage it. Let it be your slave as you walk boldly into next levels of wholeness, financial freedom and quality of life.*

**Eleven**

# Market Yourself, Like You Love Yourself

*I*f you are an entrepreneur, marketing is something that is in your blood; at least it should be there if you plan to have customers at all.

Yet, do you market your business for true success and long term benefits?

If you think that you do, you may not truly understand the true potential of the right marketing tools.

What is marketing? Marketing is what draws a customer to your business. You need to let others out there know that you are there and ready and willing to provide a service to them.

That basic definition is not nearly enough to pull you through the entire process of marketing for your business success, though.

If you want long term success, take marketing much more seriously and follow these tips for various aspects of marketing.

Determine Your Products Potential

Before you can be successful at marketing your business, you must take a good amount of time to determine what it is about what you have, that others do want.

In other words, what is it that your product provides? A successful business will offer some type of immediate satisfaction for a need that someone has. You should consider this even before you get into business. What is it that your product has the potential of solving or filling the need of?

In addition to this, you need to determine how it can offer these things to your customer in such a way as to better their life. Perhaps you can offer them something that solves a problem that they have but it still is something that is affordable to remedy that solution.

Having a clearly defined benefit to market is quite essential to getting the most from your product. People want to know, "What will it do for me?" and "Why should I purchase this over something else?"

When you can find out how this plays a role in your product's abilities, you can see the right course of marketing that product.

Answering those questions is what you must do to find defined success here.

Pricing Matters Too

The next objective to take into consideration is that of pricing. When it comes to marketing, you may not think of the price that you put onto your product, but this does matter too. People are driven by sales and deals. They like a product that can provide them with the ability to solve their need but to do so in a cost effective manner.

Without the right pricing, it makes no difference how you market the product in the end.

What are people looking for when it comes to pricing of a product or service? They want something that is fair, not something that will cause them to go broke. In addition, most people understand full well that there is a need for the business to turn a profit. The problem comes when they are being taken advantage of.

In addition, competition matters here too. If your product is better than another, perhaps it should be more, but it shouldn't be outrageous because, if it is, no one will bother with it.

Take into consideration its ability to be called a Unique Selling Proposition. This means that it will have similar but at least some unique features that will allow it to be priced in competition to other products.

Of course, as we mentioned, your product must fill the need of someone out there. But, if there are five different products doing that, it can be hard for you to find your niche. Therefore, you must create for yourself a unique quality that will propel your marketing and your pricing.

What makes your product better, in other words?

If you are a new business owner, for example, and are looking for a new product to invest in, you may not want to try to come up with your own product, own service or other component. Rather, you may just decide that taking something that is already on the market and finding a way to make it even better, or better priced, is the right way to go.

Marketing Effectively

Throughout this chapter we have talked about ways that you can market your business successfully. Now, take into consideration your sales benefits.

Can you say that when each and every one of your employees (or just yourself) walks in the door their goal is to satisfy a customer?

Not just to serve a customer but to satisfy them as well. If you can not say that, then perhaps your marketing in sales terms is not working as effectively as it should.

Here's what we mean. If you plan to set out and make a profit, then your goal is to just make the most of the business you get.

But, what if you set out to please every customer? Then, you would not only be getting that sale, but you are also getting to keep that customer coming back time and time again.

Since we are talking about long term goals and success, it makes sense to insure that your goal in sales is to be the very best at what you to in order to please your customer so much so that he does not even consider going elsewhere for his needs.

In your business, you need to keep your marketing and sales techniques focused on creating as well as keeping your customer.

Sales For Success

Taking this one step further, you also need to take into consideration your sales abilities. As a successful entrepreneur, you need to carefully consider how you are selling, how effective it is as well as how you can improve it in the short and long term.

If you can not sell, you can not be successful in your business. Point blank, you are done.

First, as the business owner, you must be able to sell yourself. Are you the business person that is:

· Approachable
· Likeable
· Friendly

· Educated
· Dedicated?

Or are you the guy they all run away from when they walk into your door? Selling yourself as a trusted resource for information and product is the best way to become the go to guy.

In addition to this, you also need to effectively sell your product to your customer. This too goes along with marketing your business for success.

In short, if you can not sell your business successfully, then you have no business in business. Learn how to be excited with your own product. Then, learn how to successfully sell it to those around you.

You need to do this first before you encourage or train someone else to do it for you. Being eager, excited, positive and surely invigorating is the way to go in this case. If you do not feel comfortable talking about your product or business to your closest friends, how in the world can you sell it to a complete stranger?

Here's the bottom line of marketing and sales. If you can not be successful at getting your product out there and getting others to see it the way that you do, then you can not possibly find success with it.

Sales expertise is essential to sales happening. Having sales; means having customers that will come back to you. That equals long term success for you, as a business owner.

## Twelve

# Ten Tips To Bring It All Together

*Principles To Remember And Use*

1. Start your business with your eyes geared towards your long term success.

2. Set and maintain goals that can be accomplished with long term objectives.

3. Manage growth carefully, without hindering your long term benefits.

4. Understand your market and how you belong in it.

5. Be the trend setter, cautiously.

6. Learn from both the good and bad of your past.

7. Invest wisely, decide wisely too.

8. Grow wisely without waste.

9. Manage your funds wisely, tightly, frugally, carefully.

10. Learn to market your business correctly, effectively.

*Tracks to Listen to While You Handle Business!*

1. Run The World, Beyoncé
2. Empire State Of Mind - Jay-Z
3. Formation - Beyoncé
4. Diva - Beyoncé
5. ApeShit - The Carters
6. Run This Town, Jay-Z
7. The Story of O.J. - Jay-Z
8. Upgrade U - Beyoncé
9. Hard Knock Life, Jay- Z
10. Heard About Us, The Carters

**Thirteen**

# Conclusion

In a world that is focused on the here and now, it is crucial for your own well being to keep an eye on your future.

When, you use wise business practices like the ones that we have talked about in this book; your goals wind up being quite beneficial. Not only can you find success for your business today, but the long term future of your business is more secured.

A business or is an investment and it very much so can go either way (good and profitable or bad and costly.) When you start out on the right foot, providing the right tools, the right knowledge and a few principles for the way that you manage your business, you find yourself having more ability to head in the positive direction of your business.

It does not matter if your business is huge and worth billions of dollars or if it a brand new business barely off its feet. The goal is to give it the nurturing principles that can help it to grow and to prosper.

If you take the time to analyze, run, and then go back again and start all over each of these aspects in your business, the end result is success.

It is your money. You can spend it any way that you want to. Using these key principles will help you to have a successful business that adds dollars to your pocket over the years by maintaining a presence in the marketplace.

# Saving A Good Girl

*Coming Fall of 2018*

Some fuckboys just can't leave well enough alone...

Amaya Adler is a bona fide boss chick, and after being hurt in her last relationship, she is completely focused on being the best mother that she can be to her son, expanding her skills, and taking her fashion design business to the next level. Even though she is determined to do her, when she meets Lucas, she is drawn into his confidence and hyper-masculinity. Being an only child, Maya has grown up getting her way and has developed a fierce stubbornness which most people couldn't handle, but Lucas, a force of nature in his own right, is turning all of that on its head.

Lucas, a successful businessman and dope boy, decided to go out on whim and let his friend fix him up. Not expecting to fall in love with Amaya, he is caught off guard when he does and sets on a course to break through her strong-willed attitude and show her what a real man can do to and for his woman.

Lucas is finally able to burst through Amaya's emotional wall and they think they're on the road to happily ever after. With everything smooth sailing, their lives are turned upside down on one fateful night that makes Lucas revert to his past and Amaya turn tail and run.

The douchebag who broke Amaya's heart has decided that he wants Amaya back. When he finds out that Lucas is the person she has moved on with, he has one goal in mind and that's to destroy her reputation so that Lucas, or any other man for that matter, will no longer want her.

Is Lucas that one person who can save Amaya and help her to heal and trust again, or will giving him a chance end up being the worst mistake of her life?

# Taming A Boss Chick

## Coming Winter 2018

Amanda Jefferson was sick and tired of being sick and tired. So, she decided to stop caring and start acting exactly like a man, as a result she went further in business and gained more satisfaction in the bedroom.

Every woman knows, that there is only so much you can give, before you chuck up the deuces, wave goodbye to your inner good girl; and start treating men the way they deserve to be treated. Just ask Amanda, she's been bad for so long that she doesn't even know what made her that way. But what she does know, is that it feels so good to have the shoe on the other foot and not have to deal with men, their feelings or their bullshit.

Not only is Amanda a Bad Girl, but she's a Boss Chick. She makes moves in the boardroom that most men wish they could and owns a tech startup; as a result, she works hard and plays harder, always keeping three men in rotation.

Why?

She needs conversation, arm candy, and good dick; in reverse order.

How does she keep it all together?

Well she has rules, and if you are trying to be a Boss Chick like Amanda take notes.

1. Work First, Play Later
2. Money over Men, Everyday
3. Never Mix Business with Pleasure

A stickler for her self-made rules, little does Amanda know, that her entire world and rule book is about to be shaken up and burned to ash when she meets Grayson Ford while on her way to an impromptu business trip. Grayson is like no other man she has ever dealt with, a force to be reckoned with in his own right with an undeniable charisma that has Amanda questioning who she is.

Deciding to put her heart on the line, Amanda open's herself up, but before they can even bask in the glow of new found love, their new relationship and a new business merger that Amanda has bet all her chips on is threatened by someone from her past, causing a far-reaching storm that shakes her life to it's very foundation.

## About the Author

Born on May 19, in Detroit, MI, Abiegail Rose is a writer, singer and motivator. Her books and podcasts focus on self-improvement, relationships, situationships, friendships, and kinships— "the ships that can sink you or take you where you need to be!" She loves filling in the black and white lines of life with dramatic colors; and she is always ready to interact with her readers and listeners.

**You can connect with me on:**
- http://abiegailrose.com
- http://twitter.com/but_amiwrong
- http://facebook.com/authorabiegailrose
- http://instagram.com/but_amiwrong

**Subscribe to my newsletter:**

✉ http://anchor.fm/butamiwrong

# Also by Abiegail Rose

**Saving A Good Girl... A Detroit Love Story**

Some fuckboys just can't leave well enough alone…

Amaya Adler is a bona fide boss chick, and after being hurt in her last relationship, she is completely focused on being the best mother that she can be to her son, expanding her skills, and taking her fashion design business to the next level. Even though she is determined to do her, when she meets Lucas, she is drawn into his confidence and hyper-masculinity…

The douchebag who broke Amaya's heart has decided that he wants Amaya back. When he finds out that Lucas is the person she has moved on with, he has one goal in mind and that's to destroy her reputation so that Lucas, or any other man for that matter, will no longer want her.

Is Lucas the one who can save a good girl, or will giving him a chance end up being the worst mistake of Amaya'life?

**Taming A Boss Chick**

Amanda Jefferson was sick and tired of being sick and tired. So, she decided to stop caring and start acting exactly like a man, as a result she went further in business and gained more satisfaction in the bedroom...

A stickler for her self-made rules, little does Amanda know, that her entire world and rule book is about to be shaken up and burned to ash when she meets Grayson Ford while on her way to an impromptu business trip. Grayson is like no other man she has ever dealt with, a force to be reckoned with in his own right with an undeniable charisma that has Amanda questioning who she is.

Deciding to put her heart on the line, Amanda open's herself up, but before they can even bask in the glow of new found love, their new relationship and a new business merger that Amanda has bet all her chips on is threatened by someone from her past, causing a far-reaching storm that shakes her life to it's very foundation.